INSIDE
COMPUTERS

BY ANGIE SMIBERT

CONTENT CONSULTANT
Ahmed Banafa
General Engineering Professor
San Jose State University

Cover image: Computers can use design software to
create models of different machines.

Core Library

An Imprint of Abdo Publishing
abdobooks.com

abdocorelibrary.com

Published by Abdo Publishing, a division of ABDO, PO Box 398166, Minneapolis, Minnesota 55439. Copyright © 2019 by Abdo Consulting Group, Inc. International copyrights reserved in all countries. No part of this book may be reproduced in any form without written permission from the publisher. Core Library™ is a trademark and logo of Abdo Publishing.

Printed in the United States of America, North Mankato, Minnesota
092018
012019

Cover Photo: Shutterstock Images
Interior Photos: Shutterstock Images, 1, 4–5; George J. McLittle/Shutterstock Images, 7, 43; iStockphoto, 10–11, 14, 19, 20, 45; Preechar Bowonkitwanchai/Shutterstock Images, 17; Syazwan Azmi/Shutterstock Images, 22–23; Kathy Willens/AP Images, 27; Red Line Editorial, 29; Patrick T. Fallon/Bloomberg/Getty Images, 32–33; STR/AFP/Getty Images, 37; J. Knaub/VivaTechnology/SIPA/AP Images, 39; Imagine China/Newscom, 40

Editor: Megan Ellis
Series Designer: Ryan Gale

Library of Congress Control Number: 2018949768

Publisher's Cataloging-in-Publication Data

Names: Smibert, Angie, author.
Title: Inside computers / by Angie Smibert.
Description: Minneapolis, Minnesota : Abdo Publishing, 2019 | Series: Inside technology | Includes online resources and index.
Identifiers: ISBN 9781532117893 (lib. bdg.) | ISBN 9781641856140 (pbk) | ISBN 9781532170751 (ebook)
Subjects: LCSH: Technological innovations--Juvenile literature. | Computer science--Juvenile literature. | Software engineering--Juvenile literature.
Classification: DDC 004--dc23

CONTENTS

WHAT MAKES A COMPUTER?

Emma types away on her laptop. She is writing a report. Music streams over the internet. It plays through speakers. Emma reads her words on the screen. She clicks a button on the trackpad. This opens the web browser. She has to do more research.

A message pops up on social media. It is from her friend Jen. Jen typed: "Help! I don't get the assignment." Emma video chats with Jen. She explains the homework. Then she goes back to her report. Emma works for another hour. Then she saves her schoolwork. She connects to her printer through Wi-Fi

Powerful computers can display advanced graphics for detailed video games, movies, and TV shows.

SUPERCOMPUTERS

Processors control a computer. The average laptop has one or two processors. A supercomputer has millions of processors. It is very powerful.

Many supercomputers are built for specific purposes. IBM's Watson is a supercomputer. It was built to answer questions asked in human languages. Watson practiced by playing the TV game show *Jeopardy!*. In 2011, Watson beat several human champions. Today, Watson is used in health care and many other areas.

and prints the report. Emma checks the clock on the computer. She has enough time to play a game before bedtime.

The laptop isn't the only computer in Emma's room. Emma has a smartphone, a tablet, a fitness tracker watch, and an e-reader. They all use computer chips.

WHAT IS A COMPUTER?

A computer is a machine. It does four basic things. First, it receives input. Input is information that comes into a computer. A keyboard, mouse, and touchscreen are some devices that create input. Second, the computer

Some computers such as laptops, *left,* can be picked up and taken other places. Other computers, called desktops, stay in one place.

processes that input. It can tell which key was pressed. Third, the computer stores this information. Finally, the computer outputs the result. It shows a letter on the screen. All of these steps happen in the blink of an eye.

The first functional modern computer was built in Germany between 1936 and 1938. It was called the Z1. It used electricity and mechanical parts to work. The first fully electronic computers were built in the 1940s. These computers were large. Each computer only did one thing. For example, during World War II (1939–1945), the British built Colossus. It was designed to break enemy codes. Colossus was the first programmable electronic computer. People manually set switches and connections. The computer read data from paper tapes.

Early computers had physical switches or bulky vacuum tubes. This controlled the electricity. Over time, computers became smaller. They also became more powerful. The transistor made this possible. A transistor is a tiny device. It controls electrical signals. It was invented in 1947.

STORED-PROGRAM COMPUTERS

In the late 1940s, mathematician John von Neumann said that computers should store programs in their memory. This would help them do many things at the same time. The first stored-program computer was the Manchester Mark 1. It was built in 1949 in Manchester, England. Most computers today store programs in their memory.

Texas Instruments introduced the integrated circuit in 1959. It is also called a microchip. The microchip made transistors smaller. They became more powerful. This made computers faster and cheaper. Emma's laptop is 1,000 times faster than one made 20 years ago.

FURTHER EVIDENCE

Chapter One introduced you to a brief history of computers. What is the main point of the chapter? What key evidence supports this point? The website below also discusses computers. Find a quote from the website that supports the main point you identified.

TIMELINE OF COMPUTER HISTORY

abdocorelibrary.com/inside-computers

HARDWARE

Hardware refers to the physical parts of a computer. There are many types of hardware. Some types are the motherboard, the CPU, memory, hard drives, and expansion boards. Many of these parts are made of circuits and transistors.

CIRCUITS AND TRANSISTORS

Electrical signals enter the computer through inputs. They leave through outputs. The computer processes those signals. It uses millions of tiny pieces. They form circuits. A simple circuit takes in a signal. It makes a change. Then it outputs the signal.

A transistor acts like a gate. It opens and closes each circuit. This happens in

A person installs a CPU into a new computer.

one billionth of a second or faster. Transistors control the electricity in the circuit.

Today's computers have microchips. Microchips are small pieces of silicon. They hold millions of transistors. Silicon is a semiconductor. It allows some electricity or heat to move through it. Some of the smallest transistors being used in 2018 were around 5 nanometers in size. A nanometer is one billionth of a meter. About 30 billion of these transistors could fit on a human fingernail.

CENTRAL PROCESSING UNIT

The CPU is the brain of the computer. It is a small circuit board. It has millions of transistors.

The CPU takes in instructions. It processes them. Then it sends output to other hardware. Some computers have many CPUs that all go on a single microchip called a core. Most computers today have more than one core.

MEMORY

Memory stores data. There are two types of memory. Random Access Memory (RAM) stores data until the computer is turned off. A laptop might have 8 gigabytes of RAM.

BITS AND BYTES

Storage and memory hold information. The amount of information is measured in units called bits and bytes. A bit is the smallest unit. One byte is equal to eight bits. A kilobyte (KB) is 1,000 bytes. A gigabyte (GB) is 1 million KB, or 1 billion bytes. Computers have different amounts of storage. For example, a laptop might have 8 GB of memory and a 1-terabyte (TB) hard drive. One TB is equal to 1,000 GB.

RAM attaches to the motherboard. Some computers have extra slots where people can add more RAM.

This is the amount of memory the computer has to keep programs and files open.

RAM comes in thin, rectangular circuit boards. RAM can be replaced or upgraded in most computers. More RAM lets the computer keep more programs open at the same time.

Another type of memory is Read-Only Memory (ROM). Most ROM cannot be changed. Some ROM helps start up the computer. This is also called booting up.

Some ROM chips are erasable. They can be programmed. Portable storage drives such as flash drives and memory cards are erasable ROM chips.

MOTHERBOARDS AND EXPANSION CARDS

The CPU, memory, and other pieces of hardware plug in to the motherboard. It is the main printed circuit board (PCB) of the computer. A PCB is a thin fiberglass board. It has electrical pathways printed on it. These pathways connect the hardware together.

Motherboards have slots for expansion cards. These are small PCBs. They help the computer do more things. Most computers come with video, audio, and networking cards. The video card controls how information shows up on the computer screen. The audio card lets the computer play and record sound. The networking card allows the computer to connect to the internet. Users can replace or upgrade most expansion cards. For example, some video games need a fast graphics card with a lot of memory.

Many video cards also have a graphics processing unit (GPU). The GPU is a microchip. It displays images and videos on the screen. A powerful GPU makes it possible to render 3D animations and video games smoothly.

Each expansion slot has a port. This connects it to an input or output device. For example, the video card has a port to connect it to the monitor with a cable. Most computers today also have universal serial bus (USB) ports. These can connect the computer to devices such as flash drives and printers.

The computer's power supply also connects to the motherboard. The power supply takes electricity from an outlet or a battery to run the computer.

STORAGE

Computers store information on drives. Today's computers have one of two kinds of storage: a hard

USB ports

The motherboard has many different cards and slots. USB ports connect the motherboard to devices such as smartphones and keyboards.

disk drive (HDD) or a solid state drive (SSD). The HDD stores data using magnets. It has a stack of metal disks. They are called platters. They are coated with iron dust. Platters spin on a spindle. They read and write data to the disk.

HDDs can be internal or external. An internal HDD is connected to the motherboard through a cable. An external HDD is connected through a USB port.

SSDs do not have moving parts. Instead, data is stored on a series of chips. SSDs can be connected to the motherboard through cables, ribbons, USB ports, or expansion slots. Some laptops have SSDs mounted directly on the motherboard. SSDs can read data faster than HDDs. But they are often more expensive.

INPUT AND OUTPUT DEVICES

Input and output devices transfer data to or from the computer. Most devices only do input or output, but some can do both.

Input devices let people put information into the computer. Many input devices are part of the computer. A touchscreen on a tablet is an input device. A laptop may have a built-in keyboard, webcam, and track pad. Other types of input devices include drawing tablets,

COMMON COMPUTER
PORTS

Ports connect the motherboard to various input or output devices. Each has a different kind of connector. Take a look at the table below. Which ports are familiar to you? Why might they have different shapes?

CONNECTOR	TYPE OF PORT
	Video Graphics Array (VGA) Used for connecting displays such as TVs or monitors
	Ethernet Used for connecting computers to a network
	Audio and Video Used for connecting devices such as DVD players and video game consoles
	USB Used for connecting devices such as keyboards, mice, and external storage
	HDMI Used for connecting high-definition displays such as TVs and monitors

A 3D printer is an output device. It receives printing instructions from a computer.

scanners, and microphones. These may connect wirelessly or through a USB port.

Output devices let the computer produce data. These devices include monitors, printers, and speakers. Hard drives, writeable CD/DVD drives, and other recordable storage are both input and output devices. They can take in input. A CD drive can read the data on a CD. They can also produce output. The CD drive can write new data such as music onto the CD.

STRAIGHT TO THE
SOURCE

In 1958, engineer Jack Kilby invented the integrated circuit. It was key in shrinking the size of computers over time. In an interview with Texas Instruments about his time working there, Kilby said:

> Well, the integrated circuit is 40 years old now and that's an incredibly long time in the history of electronics. That's longer than the vacuum tube lasted, for example. . . . [The] real story has been in the cost reduction. . . . In 1958, a single silicon transistor that was not very good sold for about $10. Today, $10 will buy something over 20 million transistors, an equal number of passive components, and all of the interconnections to make them a useful memory chip. So, the cost decrease has been factors of millions to one. And I'm sure that no one anticipated that.

> Source: Jack Kilby. "An Interview with Jack Kilby." *About Jack.* Texas Instruments, n.d. Web. Accessed July 10, 2018.

Back It Up

The author of this passage is using evidence to support a point. Write a paragraph describing the point the author is making. Then write down two or three pieces of evidence the author uses to make the point.

SOFTWARE

Software refers to the operating system and other applications, or apps, on a computer. Apps are software created to do specific tasks. Without software, the hardware couldn't do anything. Coders write software using programming languages.

OPERATING SYSTEM

Every PC has an operating system (OS). The OS is software that controls other software. It also controls some of the hardware. The OS controls how files are stored on the computer. It also lets the computer run several apps at the same time. Every app uses the CPU,

Computers can run software to edit and create movies.

23

memory, GPU, and other hardware. The OS makes sure each app runs correctly.

The OS also provides a user interface. The interface is how people interact with the computer. Some OSs include Windows, Mac, and Linux. Each OS uses a graphical user interface (GUI). A GUI displays the computer's programs and files onscreen. It uses graphics such as icons. The GUI makes it easy for the user to open files. Before GUIs, people had to type commands to run programs.

PROGRAMMING LANGUAGES

Coders use programming languages to build programs, apps, OSs, and websites. There are many programming languages. Each has rules for putting instructions together. Some languages were designed for a particular purpose. For example, languages such as C++, Java, and Python are used for many kinds of software, including video games.

APPLICATIONS

There are many different kinds of apps. They include

games, web browsers, photo editors, word processors, spreadsheets, database management, and email programs. Apps can be fun, educational, or related to work. Some types include business, graphics, communication, and security.

Some apps may come with the computer. Most computers that use Windows OS come with the Microsoft Edge web browser. Other apps need to be installed from a disc or downloaded through the internet. One popular photo editing app is Adobe Photoshop. It does not come with the computer. Today, many applications can be run without installing anything. They are stored in the cloud. The cloud is remote storage that uses the internet. Email accounts use cloud storage to store emails and files.

BUSINESS APPS

Business apps, or productivity apps, help people do tasks for work or school. They help users write reports, create presentations, and crunch numbers.

They also include software for making spreadsheets and scheduling appointments.

A word processor is one of the most popular types of app. It creates documents with text and graphics. The user types a few letters. The app sends instructions to the CPU. The CPU sends instructions to the monitor. Then the monitor displays the results on the screen.

GRAPHICS APPS

People use graphics apps to create and edit images. These apps include drawing, photo editing, animation, and movie software. They use the GPU to display and edit images. Many computers come with simple graphics apps. Professional artists often buy more complex apps that do not come with the computer.

Graphics apps create two types of graphic images. They are called vector and raster. A vector image is based on math. Lines and shapes can be shown with a mathematical formula. When someone draws a line with the mouse, an app saves the formula that the

Photoshop is one type of graphics app. Many people who create and edit images use Photoshop.

line makes. Some apps can make complicated vector graphics. They have many formulas. Vector graphics can be made larger and smaller. They do not lose any quality.

Raster graphics are made up of tiny dots. These dots are called pixels. They store information about the image. Raster graphics lose quality when they are made larger. They are created at a certain size. Each image has a specific number of pixels per square inch.

When someone takes a photo with a camera, she chooses the size of the photo. It is measured in pixels. A high-resolution photo might be 1920 x 1080 pixels. But if the photo is made larger, the pixels do not get larger. The software tries to fill in some of the gaps. This makes a blurry image.

OPEN SOURCE SOFTWARE

Open source software is software anyone can change and share. Most software is designed so that only its authors can change it. Open source software is different. Its authors make the code available to anyone. They want other people to learn from, improve, and share the source code. Some examples of open source software include the Linux operating system, Open Office, Firefox, Audacity, and GIMP.

COMMUNICATION APPS

Communication apps give us ways to interact with other people over the internet. These apps include web browsers, social media, email, messaging, and video chat.

A web browser is an app that lets the user access the World

MUSIC STREAMING
APPS

In the past, people had to purchase individual songs to listen to them. As of 2018, millions of people use music streaming apps. People play music over the internet instead of downloading songs. Some apps are free. They may have commercials between songs. Other apps cost a monthly fee and do not have commercials. The graph below shows the most popular streaming apps in the United States as of March 2018. Why might so many people use music streaming apps? Why do you think people might still pay for individual songs?

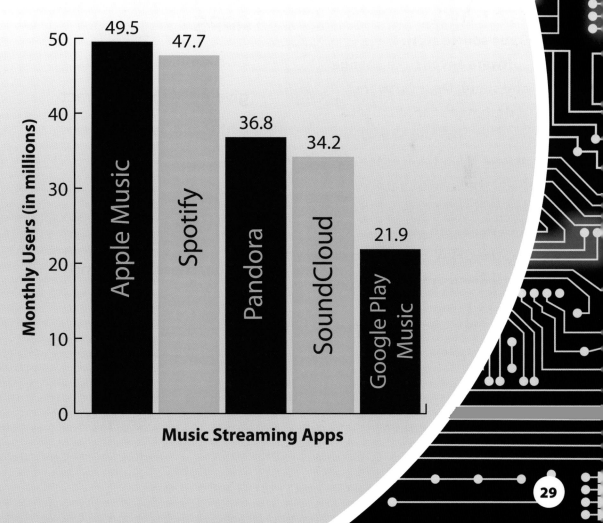

Wide Web. The World Wide Web is part of the internet. It is a system of linked websites. Websites include everything from online stores to social media to video streaming services. Popular web browsers are Microsoft Edge, Safari, Chrome, Opera, and Firefox. Most web browsers are free to download.

Email and messaging apps let people talk to each other. Email apps let users send and receive messages. Users can email each other with an app or online through a website. Messaging apps let users chat individually or in groups. Some apps, such as Instagram and Facebook Messenger, also let people video chat. Other apps such as Skype are designed specifically for video chatting.

SECURITY APPS

People need software to keep their computers safe. Security apps protect the computer from attacks by hackers who might use computer viruses and other malware. Malware is short for malicious software. It is any program that is created to damage a computer. A computer virus is a piece of code. It can copy itself. Then it infects a computer. Antivirus software scans the computer. It disables any viruses it finds.

People also have apps for playing music, audiobooks, podcasts, and videos. They might also download or buy software to edit their own movies and music. Many people play games. Others might have software for building their own websites. The possibilities for software are endless.

EXPLORE ONLINE

Chapter Three discusses different types of operating systems, including Linux. This article in *Wired* explains why Linux is used on many popular devices such as tablets and Android phones. Does the article answer any questions you had about the OS?

LINUX TOOK OVER THE WEB. NOW, IT'S TAKING OVER THE WORLD
abdocorelibrary.com/inside-computers

THE FUTURE OF COMPUTERS

Computers have gotten smaller, faster, and more powerful over the last 50 years. As of 2018, the smallest transistors on the market are around 10 nanometers. Scientists are working on transistors that are only 2 to 3 nanometers across. Many experts do not think transistors can keep shrinking. Computer and chip makers might have to get creative to keep improving computers. This may mean using new materials or finding new ways of computing.

NEW SEMICONDUCTORS

Most chips in 2018 are made of silicon. Another option may be graphene, which is

At a 2018 trade show, Dell displayed a circuit board that was made with recycled gold.

also a semiconductor. It is clear, flexible, and incredibly strong. It is a better semiconductor than silicon.

Another option is carbon nanotubes. They are long, thin molecules of carbon. They are shaped like tubes. The tubes are only one to three nanometers across. They are also semiconductors.

Graphene chips might be faster and hold more transistors. Carbon nanotube chips might be smaller. However, these materials are incredibly thin. They are hard to work with. Researchers are still looking for ways to build computers using them.

DEEP LEARNING

In recent years, artificial intelligence (AI) research has made many advances. AI assistants such as Alexa and Siri can understand spoken words. AI can help doctors spot illnesses. It can even run self-driving cars.

AIs are programmed to do certain tasks. But they aren't programmed for everything that could happen while doing those tasks. Instead, the AIs learn how to improve what they do. They can even teach themselves. This is called machine learning. It happens because of a neural net. A neural net is software inspired by the human brain. It mimics how we think brain cells work.

Neural nets are not new. But scientists have been able to build neural nets with more and more layers. This has led to deep learning. Deep learning allows AIs to learn more things. The hardware does not have to change. The software does the work. In 2016, Google's AlphaGo AI taught itself to play the game Go. The game is

ARTIFICIAL INTELLIGENCE

People often see AI as a "thinking machine." They think the computer imitates human thought. Researchers are divided on how they define AI. Some want to build a computer that thinks like a human. This is called Strong AI. So far, it has been hard to do. All AI as of 2018 was Weak AI. AI software is trained to do specific tasks through machine learning. It may recognize spoken language, drive a car, or play *Jeopardy!*. AI assistants like Siri and Alexa are examples of Weak AI.

hard to master. But the AI beat one of the world's best human players.

BIOCOMPUTING

Scientists are engineering living cells to act as computers. They are programming cells to form circuits using DNA. DNA is a material in all living cells. It carries genetic information. In 2017, researchers at Harvard Medical School programmed a tiny movie into a cell of bacteria. They converted the pixels into the DNA code and were able to read the code to recreate the movie. Researchers from Boston University built genetic circuits in a cell from a mammal in 2017. In the future, biocomputers might be used to fight tumors or other diseases in the body.

QUANTUM COMPUTING

Another innovative type of computer is the quantum computer. It uses quantum theory to process information. Quantum theory describes how energy and matter act at the very smallest level. This is the

In 2016, the AlphaGo AI beat the world's best Go player, Ke Jie, after three rounds. In the future AI may be able to do more complicated tasks that humans cannot do.

atomic level. At that level, scientists can't be sure of anything. According to quantum theory, we can know exactly where an electron is or how fast it's going.

SPACEBORNE COMPUTER

In September 2017, a supercomputer called the Spaceborne Computer was installed in the International Space Station. It is part of a test to see how supercomputers work in space. Radiation in space causes technology to degrade over time. But the Spaceborne Computer protects itself from radiation. When it senses a lot of radiation, it slows down its operating speed. This helps it avoid damage.

The Spaceborne Computer does 1 trillion calculations per second. This is 30 times faster than a standard laptop. Supercomputers in space may provide high quality images of planets in the solar system. They may also help us communicate with astronauts traveling to Mars.

We cannot know both. This is called the Uncertainty Principle.

Quantum computing can be used for calculating very large numbers. This is helpful in encryption and code breaking. People have talked about quantum computing for years. But the computers are still being developed. In 2018, IBM announced a computer system that could handle 49 quantum bits (qubits) of information.

IBM has started the IBM Q initiative to help people research quantum computing. As of 2018, quantum computers, shown above, are still in testing.

These systems would be available through their cloud storage system.

Moore's Law may come to an end soon. But experts think computers will continue to change and improve. Neural nets have changed how computers work.

In Hangzhou, China, a restaurant uses facial recognition software to charge people for the meals they ordered.

Quantum and biological computers may change our understanding of what computers are. Microchips might be made of something other than silicon. New materials may revolutionize transistors. Or some new invention might replace the transistor. Whatever forms they take, computers will continue to take in input, process it, store it, and then create amazing output.

STRAIGHT TO THE
SOURCE

Stephen Hawking was the director of research at the Centre for Theoretical Cosmology in Cambridge, England. He was concerned about the rise in AI technology. In an article in the *Independent*, Hawking and other scientists wrote:

> Success in creating AI would be the biggest event in human history.
>
> Unfortunately, it might also be the last, unless we learn how to avoid the risks. In the near term, world militaries are considering autonomous-weapon systems that can choose and eliminate targets; the UN and Human Rights Watch have advocated a treaty banning such weapons. . . . AI may transform our economy to bring both great wealth and great dislocation.
>
> Source: Stephen Hawking et al. "Stephen Hawking: 'Transcendence Looks at the Implications of Artificial Intelligence.'" *Independent*. Independent, May 1, 2014. Web. Accessed June 4, 2018.

Consider Your Audience

Adapt this passage for a different audience, such as your principal or friends. Write a blog post conveying this same information for the new audience. How does your post differ from the original text and why?

FAST FACTS

- A computer takes in input, processes it, stores it, and then outputs the results.

- The first computers used vacuum tubes to control the flow of electricity. The transistor was invented in 1947. It made the vacuum tube obsolete.

- Hardware refers to the physical parts of the computer.

- A circuit takes in a signal, changes it, and then outputs it.

- A transistor is a tiny device that works as a gate to open and close circuits.

- Today's computers use integrated circuits. They hold millions of transistors.

- The motherboard is a large printed circuit board that connects the computer's internal hardware.

- Software tells the hardware what to do. Software includes programs, applications, and the operating system (OS).

- The OS manages the computer's hardware as well as the other software.

- Programs and applications let the user do specific tasks.

- Coders use programming languages to write software.

- Graphene and carbon nanotubes are two possible replacements for silicon in transistors.

- Biological computing uses living matter such as DNA to process information.

STOP AND
THINK

You Are There

Chapter One discusses the history of computers. Imagine you are working on the Colossus computers in 1943 to break secret codes. Write a letter telling your friends about the computers and your work. What do you notice about the computers? Be sure to add plenty of detail to your notes.

Dig Deeper

After reading this book, what questions do you still have about programming languages? With an adult's help, find a few reliable sources that can help you answer your questions. Write a paragraph about what you learned.

Say What?

Studying computers can mean learning a lot of new vocabulary. Find five words in this book you've never heard before. Use a dictionary to find out what they mean. Then write the meanings in your own words, and use each word in a new sentence.

Take a Stand

Chapter Four talks about the future of AI. Some people are excited for AI programs to do more tasks. Others are worried that AI might become too powerful, or that people might use AI to do bad things. Do you think people would benefit from more AI? Or do you think more AI would be dangerous? Why?

GLOSSARY

bit
a single unit of computer information

circuit
the complete path an electric current travels along

genetic
something that passes down features from one organism to another

hard drive
a device that is used for storing computer data

microchip
a group of circuits that work together on a very small piece of material such as silicon

neural net
software inspired by the human brain

pixel
a small dot that comes together with other pixels to form raster images on computer monitors

render
to show an image on a computer

semiconductor
a material or object that allows some electricity or heat to move through it and that is used especially in electronic devices

transistor
a small device that is used to control the flow of electricity in electronics

ONLINE
RESOURCES

To learn more about computers, visit our free resource websites below.

Visit **abdocorelibrary.com** for free Common Core resources for teachers and students, including vetted activities, multimedia, and booklinks, for deeper subject comprehension.

Visit **abdobooklinks.com** for free additional online weblinks for further learning. These links are routinely monitored and updated to provide the most current information available.

LEARN
MORE

Computer Coding. New York: DK Publishing, 2014.

Conley, Kate. *Inside Drones*. Minneapolis: Abdo, 2019.

INDEX

About the Author

Angie Smibert was a science writer and online training developer at NASA's Kennedy Space Center. She currently teaches writing for Indiana University as well as Southern New Hampshire University.